This book belongs to

chris gist

5000 sudbury way
483-4006
Carmichael, Calif. 95608

D0646528

FAMOUS

INDIAN TRIBES

by **WILLIAM MOYERS** *and* **DAVID C. COOKE**

Illustrated by WILLIAM MOYERS

RANDOM HOUSE, NEW YORK

This title was originally catalogued by the Library of Congress as follows:

Moyers, William
    Famous Indian tribes.   By William Moyers and David
C. Cooke.   Illus. by William Moyers.   Random House
ᶜ1954
    64p col illus 29 cm
    An introduction to the way some Indian tribes lived,
their wars, and their great chiefs.
    1 Indians of North America—History I Cooke, David
C., joint author II Title

Trade Ed.: ISBN: 394-80651-4   Lib. Ed.: ISBN: 394-90651-9

THE INDIANS AND
THE PILGRIMS

THERE were many different kinds of Indians living in this country when the white men first came here.

Some of the Indians were very friendly people. Their kindness made it possible for the Pilgrims to survive their very first winter in the new land.

When the Pilgrims had a feast to thank God for His help, they invited their Indian friends to join in the celebration of the first Thanksgiving Day.

3

THE FOREST INDIANS

SOME of the largest and most important Indian tribes once lived in the northeastern and southeastern parts of our country. They were scattered as far west as the Great Lakes and ranged from Maine all the way down to Florida.

Among the tribes in the northeastern part were the Iroquois, Delaware, Shawnee, Huron, Erie, Miami, Ottawa, Wampanoag, Sauk, and Kickapoo. The Iroquois included the following tribes: Mohawk, Oneida, Onondaga, Cayuga, and Seneca.

Many of the Indians who lived in the cold northern sections made homes called wigwams. These were generally oval in shape and had frameworks of poles covered with bark. There was only one doorway in a wigwam, but the Indians left a hole in the middle of the roof so that the smoke from their fires could escape.

Slightly different types of homes were used by the Creeks, Chick-asaws, Cherokees, and other tribes who lived in the warm southern sections of the country.

Indians had dances for almost everything—war dances, dances to chase away evil spirits, dances to thank their gods for good crops or good hunting, and many other kinds.

Forest Indians usually built their villages on the banks of rivers and used canoes whenever they wanted to travel.

The tribes in the South built heavy canoes. To make them, the Indians first burned down trees and then hollowed them out by building fires on the logs. The burned wood was then scraped away with stone axes. It took a long time to make these canoes, and when

they were finished they were so heavy that two or three strong men were needed to lift them.

The tribes in the North built canoes that were light enough to be carried. First they made a framework of branches tied together with strips of leather. Then they covered it with tree bark such as birch.

Hunting and fishing were the duties of the men. It was their job to supply the people with fresh meat, and to fight their enemies in time of war. These were very important tasks, and young boys were given long training so that they would grow up to be good hunters and warriors.

When a boy was old enough to start his training, his father would take him to the forest each day and teach him the things he had to know.

Indian boys learned how to shoot their bows and arrows. They learned how to move through the woods so quietly that an animal or an enemy could not hear them. They learned to track animals or human beings by watching for such signs as overturned stones or leaves or broken twigs. The boys became so good at reading forest signs that they could look at a footprint in the earth and tell how long ago it had been made.

The boys also learned how to leave signs to show their friends which way they had traveled. They learned to imitate the sounds of game animals.

Pounding corn into meal

While the boys were busy in the forests, the girls, too, were learning many useful skills. They had to know how to skin animals and smoke the meat so that it would not spoil through the long winter months. They had to know how to tan skins to make them soft enough to be made into clothing. They had to learn to take care of vegetable gardens, to grind corn into meal, to weave baskets, and to make pots from clay.

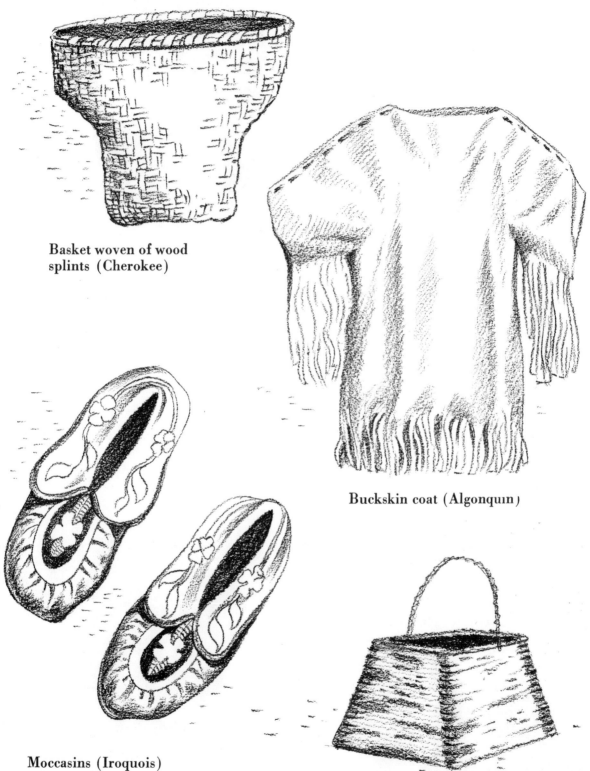

Basket woven of wood
splints (Cherokee)

Buckskin coat (Algonquın)

Moccasins (Iroquois)

Birch bark water vessel
(Iroquois)

Some of the great
chiefs among the
Forest Indians

HIAWATHA
(Onondaga)

According to legend, Hiawatha of the Onondaga tribe was a great man. He is said to have persuaded the Mohawks, Oneidas, Onondagas, Cayugas, and Senecas to join together and promise to help one another. Years later the Tuscaroras moved up from the South and joined them. These tribes were called The Six Nations of the Iroquois.

RED JACKET
(Seneca)

LITTLE TURTLE
(Miami)

There were many other great chiefs among the Forest Indians. Some of these were Little Turtle, Red Jacket, Pontiac, King Philip, Black Hawk, and Keokuk.

KING PHILIP
(Wampanoag)

PONTIAC
(Ottawa)

BLACK HAWK
(Sauk)

KEOKUK
(Sauk)

TECUMSEH

Perhaps the most famous of the chiefs in the northern section of the country was Tecumseh, of the Shawnee tribe, who lived from 1768 to 1813. Tecumseh tried to convince the white men that the Indians should be allowed to form their own nation. The white men did not agree. As a result, there was a bloody battle and the red men were badly beaten by General Harrison and his soldiers.

16

Another great Indian was the Cherokee, Sequoyah, who lived from 1770 to 1843. Although he was a cripple and unable to hunt with the others in his tribe, he was a man of great brilliance. The greatest tree that grows in the United States—the giant sequoia—was named after him.

Sequoyah saw white men writing messages to each other, and he decided to invent an alphabet for his people so that they, too, would be able to read and write.

SEQUOYAH

He worked for twelve years before he finally completed an alphabet that was simple enough for all his people to learn. Within a few months after the alphabet was given to the Cherokees, almost all of them could read and write.

The most famous of the chiefs in the south was Osceola, leader of the Seminoles of Florida. (These were members of the Creek tribe.)

Spain sold Florida to the United States in 1819, and one of the terms of the sale was that the Seminoles would not be harmed. This promise was never kept, and hundreds of Indians were captured and forced to work as slaves.

When the United States ordered that all Seminoles were to be moved to Oklahoma, Osceola led his people into the swamplands. With that move, the war was on!

The Americans lost a great number of men and spent many thousands of dollars trying to defeat the Seminoles, but they never succeeded.

Some of the Seminoles never surrendered to the white men, and their descendants still live in the swamps of Florida much as their ancestors did more than a hundred years ago.

THE PLAINS INDIANS

THE Indians who dwelt on the great plains between the Mississippi River and the Rocky Mountains lived mainly by hunting the buffalo. Among them were the Blackfeet, Cheyennes, the Comanches, the Crows, the Arapahos, and the Sioux.

The Plains Indians used shorter bows than those of the Forest Hunters, but these bows were powerful enough to shoot an arrow that would kill a buffalo. Even after they got guns from the white men in exchange for furs, many of the Indians still preferred to hunt with bow and arrow.

There was always a great celebration after a successful buffalo hunt. There would be dances to thank the Great Spirit for his help, and then all the people would feast on roasted fresh buffalo meat.

During the feast the warriors told stories of the hunt and how they had finally killed one of the great beasts. If a boy had killed his first buffalo, his mother and father told everyone how proud they were of his bravery. Then they made him give the meat from his animal to the family of a warrior who had not been so lucky. In this way, the boy learned to share whatever he had with less fortunate people.

The buffalo was the most important thing in the world to these Indians. They used buffalo meat for their main food; they used the hides to make rope, cooking pots, and covers for their tepees. They used buffalo horns and bones for tools and weapons, and they used the hoofs to make glue. Not a single part of the huge animal was thrown away.

Scraping the skins of buffaloes

ARTICLES MADE FROM THE BUFFALO

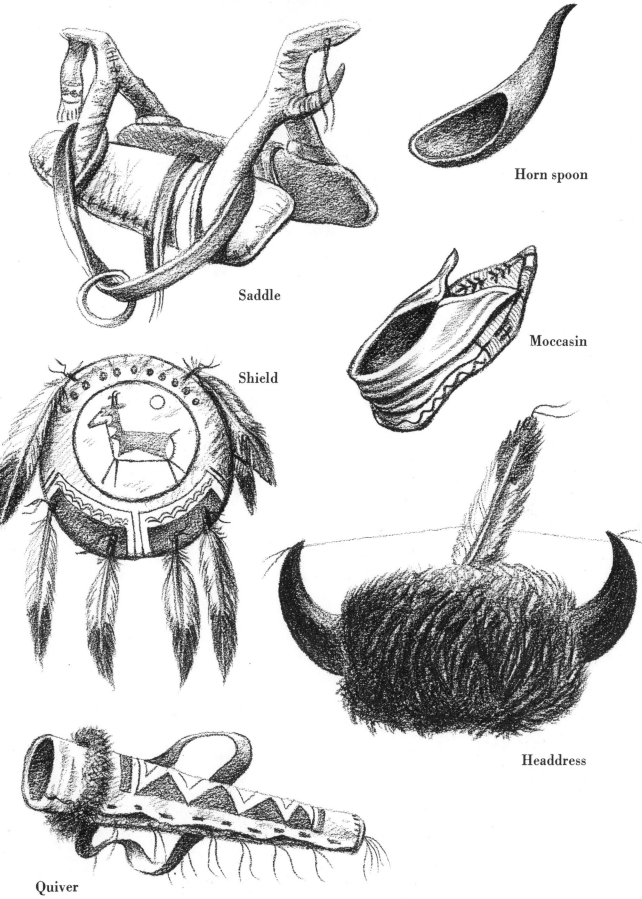

Horn spoon

Saddle

Shield

Moccasin

Headdress

Quiver

The Plains Indians often made fancy war bonnets of eagle feathers and buffalo skin, but only the bravest warriors could wear them. Each feather in a bonnet had a special meaning and could be earned only in war. Some feathers meant that the warrior was one of the first men to charge into battle. Some meant that he had captured enemy warriors. Others meant that he had touched an enemy with his bare hands without killing the man.

These honors were very hard for an Indian to earn. It took a great deal of courage to win the highest honors, and many warriors lost their lives in trying to do so.

The chief of a tribe usually decided which of his warriors were brave enough to get certain types of feathers, and these were awarded with great ceremony, just as medals are given to soldiers today. One of the highest honors was given to warriors who brought back eagle feathers to be placed in war bonnets, for hunting these birds was hard and dangerous.

26

The kind of shelter used by the Plains Indians was the tepee. This tentlike house made it possible for the tribesmen to follow a buffalo herd without having to build new homes every time they set up camp. Some of the tepees were as big across as the living room in a modern house and were covered with as many as forty buffalo skins that had been sewn together.

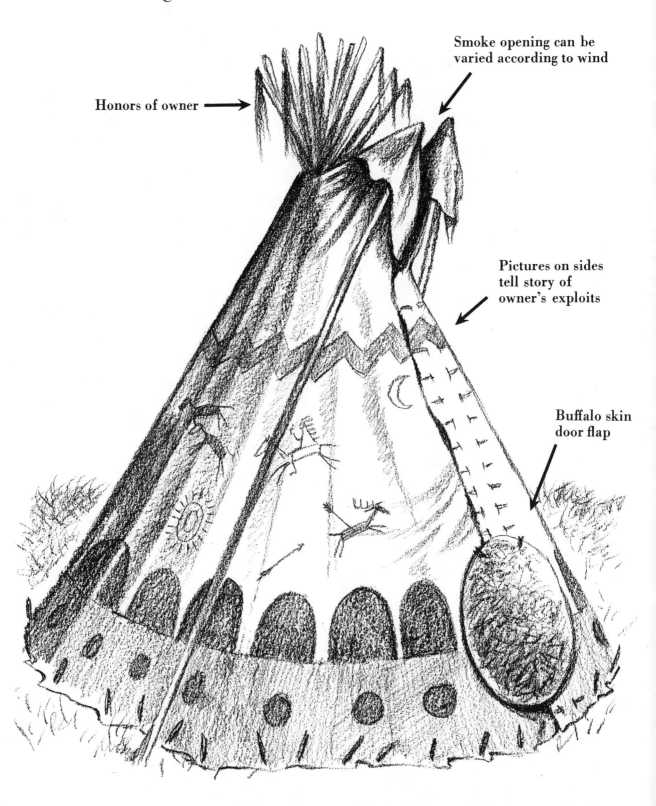

Honors of owner →

Smoke opening can be varied according to wind

Pictures on sides tell story of owner's exploits

Buffalo skin door flap

Tepees were not only good for traveling but also made very comfortable living quarters. The flap-door could be closed when winter winds blew across the plains, and a fire could be built in the middle of the tepee floor. In the summer the sides could be rolled up to let the air blow through.

The Plains Indians also used the system of smoke signals. This system worked particularly well where they lived, for puffs of smoke billowing into the air could be seen for many miles across the flat land. The Indians made the smoke by covering their signal fires with grass or branches that were not dried out. First the smoke would be held down with blankets. When the blankets were suddenly raised, the smoke would rise in puffs. By sending up fast or slow puffs, the Indians could transmit almost any message to their friends, just as today we send telegraph messages by dots and dashes.

Most of the Plains Indians were enemies of the white men not only because they wanted to protect their lands but also because the settlers killed off the buffaloes in such great numbers. Did you know that William Cody was given the nickname "Buffalo Bill" because he was said to have killed more than four hundred buffaloes in a single day?

RED CLOUD

Sometimes the feelings between the white men and the Plains Indians would become so bitter that a war would start. One of the biggest wars against the whites was led by Red Cloud, a Sioux chief who was the leader of more than three thousand warriors in the northern part of Wyoming.

Sitting Bull, another Sioux chief, is famous as the leader of the Indians who killed General Custer and his men in the battle of the Little Big Horn.

Still another great chief was Joseph of the Nez Percé tribe. The Nez Percés were among the most peaceful of all Indian tribes, and until 1877 they had never killed a white man. But when Chief Joseph finally went on the warpath, he turned out to be such a clever general that his battles were later studied by West Point cadets.

THE DESERT INDIANS

THE Southwest, where the states of Arizona and New Mexico are located, was the land of some of the most famous Indian tribes on our continent. Among them were the Apaches, the greatest of all fighting tribes.

Names like Mangas Coloradas, Cochise, Victorio, Nana, Geronimo, and Loco struck fear into the hearts of white men.

Victorio, Loco, Nana, and Geronimo were members of Mangas Coloradas' tribe. After their chief was killed, these warriors continued their war against the white men until 1886, when Geronimo finally surrendered because his band of braves was too worn out to fight any longer.

39

Strangely enough, the Southwest was also the home of the most peaceful of Indians—the Hopis and Pueblos and Zunis. These people were farmers and weavers who went to live in the caves and openings high on the walls of steep cliffs where they could not be attacked.

Although centuries have passed since people made their homes

in cliff dwellings, they were so well built that many of them are still in existence. These remains are cared for by our government as national monuments. Among the many places where they may be visited is Mesa Verde National Park in southwest Colorado, which has more than three hundred cliff dwellings.

The Navahos, another desert tribe, did not live in cities as the Pueblos did. They moved from place to place so that their sheep would always have good pasture.

The Navahos made their homes in small earth-covered huts called hogans.

The rugs and blankets the Navahos make from the wool of their sheep are more beautiful than those woven by any other group of Indians. No two rugs or blankets are ever exactly the same, even though they may look very much alike. Then, too, there is always a small mistake in the design of the rug or blanket. This is deliberately because of the Navaho woman's belief that she must never do a perfect job or her life on earth will be finished.

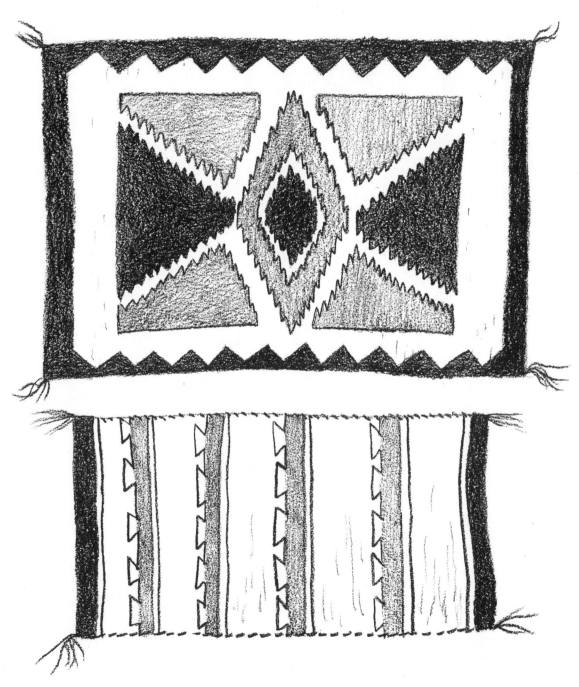

It was Kit Carson, the famous Indian fighter, who brought the Navahos under the control of the United States. He marched into their lands in 1864 with four hundred soldiers, ready for war if the Indians decided to fight. Only a very small number of the Navahos tried to stop the whites, and they were killed. The others gave up peacefully and were sent to live on a reservation.

ACORN EATERS

THE Indians who lived in California and the southern part of Oregon had a way of life that was very simple and primitive. Among these were the Hupas, Klamaths, Umatillas, Modocs, and the Pomos.

Strange as it may seem, the main food of most of these tribes was acorns. They ate game and shellfish too, for they often hunted and fished.

These people did not have horses, and since there was no reason for them to travel long distances they did not always build real canoes.

If they wanted to cross a lake or a river, they sometimes made wooden rafts or used large waterproof baskets for boats. Some of the tribes had boats that looked a little like canoes. These were called balsas and were made of long bundles of reeds tied tightly together.

THE WOODCARVERS AND

FISHERMEN

ON a narrow strip of land that stretches along the Pacific Coast from southern Oregon to Alaska, there lived Indians whose customs were much different from those of other tribes. Among them were the Bella Coolas, the Haidas, the Nootkas, the Kwakiutls, and the Tlingits. The members of these tribes were fishermen and wood-carvers.

They lived mainly on fish, for the waters in that section were, and still are, the greatest spawning grounds in the world. In the spring of the year thousands and thousands of salmon make their way into

the rivers from the ocean, fighting upstream to the still waters where they lay their eggs.

As the fish leaped up waterfalls and over rocks and through shallow water, the Indians would spear them or scoop them up with nets. In a few days the Indians were able to catch enough fish to last the tribe for many months.

The people in this section could not live in the kinds of homes used by other Indians. Where there was so much rain, tepees would have soon rotted, and earth-covered hogans or pueblos would have been washed away. For this reason, the tribes in that area made permanent homes of wood. Some of these were more than fifty feet long and housed several families.

A house sometimes took many years to build, for these Indians took pride in their work and wanted it to be perfect. If a family moved, the house was taken apart and carried along to be set up as their new home. When a man died, the house became his son's

property, and he, in turn, would pass it on to *his* son. The houses were built so well that ruins of some of them are still standing today.

These Indians were famous for the beautifully carved and painted totem poles which they set in front of their homes. Totem poles were not made to frighten evil spirits, as many people believe, but rather to tell the history of a family. Every person in a family had the name of some animal—eagle, bear, wolf, owl, whale, and many others—and the faces of these animals were often carved in the totem poles. Each house in a village had at least one totem pole in front of it. The totem poles of the Haida tribes were often so large that holes big enough to be used as doorways could be cut in them.

The Indians along the north Pacific Coast were also famous for their canoes. Different types of canoes were built for traveling in different waters. Small canoes were used only on rivers and lakes.

Larger canoes that could carry as many as fifty people were used on the rough ocean waters.

The Nootkas went after whales and seals and porpoises as well as salmon. Several canoes, each with a crew of eight men, were needed on whaling trips. The men paddled many miles out into the ocean and were away for days at a time. For this reason each canoe carried a supply of food and drinking water.

These Indians did not make pottery, but they wove beautiful baskets and blankets. The blankets were made of strange mixtures of cedarwood bark, mountain-goat wool, and dog hair, but they were warm and colorful. Members of the tribes also used cedar bark and spruce roots to make wide-brimmed hats which were woven so tightly that they could be worn in rainy weather.

Ceremonial Masks

Straw rain hat

Ceremonial blanket

WHERE ARE THE TRIBES TODAY?

MOST Indian tribes have remained on the land set aside for them by the government. Some of these reservations are in the part of the country in which the people originally lived, but most of them are not. For a long time the Indians were moved from their own lands to discourage them from fighting again. That is why some eastern tribes are found in Oklahoma and some mountain tribes are found on dry plains.

Many of the tribes were given poor land for reservations, but in some cases this land has become very valuable. Oil was discovered on two or three reservations, gold was located on others. Today uranium is being found in the barren reservations of Oklahoma and in the Navaho country. These discoveries have made a few of the tribes very wealthy, but others still have a hard time finding enough to eat. To exist, they must count on help from the United States government.

Indians are being educated in the schools that have been built for them. There are hospitals where they may be protected against disease and cured when they are sick. In 1934 a law was passed giving the Indians the right to govern themselves. The law also promised loans of money to tribes that wanted to go into business. Many tribes asked for and received loans.

Every one of the tribes has been able to repay its loan.

The old customs have passed away with most of the Indians, but in some tribes they are still strong. A large number of the Hopis and Zunis still live in pueblos and make pottery and farm their old lands. Many of the Navahos still live in earth-covered hogans and make blankets and have their own medicine men. If you visit some of these reservations today you will find the Indians living much as their ancestors did hundreds of years ago.

In 1924 all Indians in the United States were declared citizens and were given the right to vote. A large number of them were in the Army and Navy during World War II, and they fought for this country just as bravely as their grandfathers and great-grandfathers fought against the white men long ago.

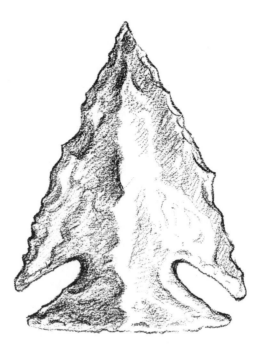

Arrowhead

RANDOM HOUSE BOOKS FOR CHILDREN

Question and Answer Books

For ages 6-10:
Question and Answer Book of Nature
Question and Answer Book of Science
Question and Answer Book of Space
Question and Answer Book About the
   Human Body

Gateway Books

For ages 8 and up:
The Friendly Dolphins
The Horse that Swam Away
Champ: Gallant Collie
Mystery of the Musical Umbrella
and other titles

Step-Up Books

For ages 7-8:
Animals Do the Strangest Things
Birds Do the Strangest Things
Fish Do the Strangest Things
Meet Abraham Lincoln
Meet John F. Kennedy
and other titles

Babar Books

For ages 4 and up:
The Story of Babar
Babar the King
The Travels of Babar
Babar Comes to America
and other titles

Books by Dr. Seuss

For ages 5 and up:
Dr. Seuss's Sleep Book
Happy Birthday to You!
Horton Hatches the Egg
Horton Hears a Who
If I Ran the Zoo
I Had Trouble in Getting to Solla
   Sollew
McElligot's Pool
On Beyond Zebra
Scrambled Eggs Super!
The Sneetches
Thidwick: The Big-Hearted Moose
Yertle the Turtle
and other titles

Giant Picture Books

For ages 5 and up:
Abraham Lincoln
Big Black Horse
Big Book of Things to Do and
   Make
Big Book of Tricks and Magic
Blue Fairy Book
Daniel Boone
Famous Indian Tribes
George Washington
Hiawatha
King Arthur
Peter Pan
Robert E. Lee
Robin Hood
Robinson Crusoe
Three Little Horses
Three Little Horses at the King's
   Palace

Beginner Books

For ages 5-7:
The Cat in the Hat Beginner Book
   Dictionary
The Cat in the Hat
The Cat in the Hat Comes Back
Dr. Seuss's ABC Book
Green Eggs and Ham
Go, Dog, Go!
Bennett Cerf's Book of Riddles
The King, the Mice and the Cheese
and other titles

Picture Books

For ages 4 and up:
Poems to Read to the Very Young
Songs to Sing with the Very Young
Stories to Read to the Very Young
Alice in Wonderland
Anderson's Fairy Tales
Bambi's Children
Black Beauty
Favorite Tales for the Very Young
Grandmas and Grandpas
Grimm's Fairy Tales
Heidi
Little Lost Kitten
Mother Goose
Once-Upon-A-Time Storybook
Pinocchio
Puppy Dog Tales
Read-Aloud Nursery Tales
Sleeping Beauty
The Sleepytime Storybook
Stories that Never Grow Old
The Wild and Wooly Animal Book
The Wizard of Oz

RANDOM HOUSE, INC., 457 MADISON AVENUE, NEW YORK 22, N.Y.